Stand Tall, Stand Strong

Damien Bryan

BookLeaf Publishing

Presentation by *BookLeaf Publishing*

Web: www.bookleafpub.com

E-mail: info@bookleafpub.com

ISBN: 978-93-95890-14-4

First edition 2022

Dedicated to all those who strain and struggle to succeed; theirs is a strength the world seldom sees.

ACKNOWLEDGEMENT

This book of poetry would not have been possible without the unwavering support of a few close friends and family, they know who they are - thank you for letting me spam you with so much writing!

Books & Covers

Dark is my mind, but bright is my face.
Wide is my smile that betrays no trace,
Of the demons that lurk and skulk and race
To invade quiet thoughts – my haunted space.

I can do more than you ask – better than you
think.
But sometimes, when I try to swim, I suddenly
sink.
My brain has the words, but my mouth has no
ink,
And then it begins…I overthink.

Sinking

2

There's so much water, water everywhere,
I can feel my body starting to sink.
My neck strains back as my eyes blankly stare
In quiet fear struggling on the brink.
As water melts through my gripping fingers,
I wonder how I will remain afloat.
As I drown in the deep blue, time lingers
Ever longer, washing away my hope.
Now muffled screams drowned out my final cry,
As my thrashing and splashing diminished.
Tired and weak my mind now says goodbye,
As my all-too-short fight for life finished.
      Submerged now completely and out of breath,
      There's nothing for me but silence and death.

Retweeted Rhymes

Hickory, dickory, dock;
slave to Snapchat, Insta, TikTok.

Little Jane Peep got no sleep;
anxious for likes from online sheep

Hey diddle, diddle, her looks
she did fiddle, to become Miss-guided dream.

Twinkle, twinkle, little star –
she'll post online without the scar.

Jane be nimble, Jane be quick;
don't cut deep; just a little nick.

Sticks and stones may break her bones
but their words did quietly crush her.

Quiet thoughts make the most noise

We all have demons, ghosts and nightmares
that crawl from the dark when we think no one
cares.
They fester and plot, dripping disdain,
feeding off quiet, internalized pain
that nobody sees, but results they can watch.
As it all spills out, you're overcome; awash,

with irrational thoughts, those three concoct,
like fast-flowing paint, your pages they blot.
Caught in their eddy you're spiralling down;
no laughter or joy, just the tears of a clown.
Grasping for rope and gasping for air,
you call and you call, but nobody's there.

Or at least no one who hears with the heart, not
their head.
And can read between lines to infer all you've
not said.
So further you're sucked and sink in the sand,

soul's fallen over; its dark dreams make you
stand.
At least for as long as it takes them to break:
your love… your spirit… 'til you make last
mistake.

So, greet you I will or offence you may take;
I'll say hi, how are ya, and give a damn's sake.
And spend a quiet moment to properly look,
not just read front cover of well-marketed book.
I'll give you free time over immeasurable drink,
that puts arm on a shoulder to pull you back
from the brink.

It's the small things that matter to which we pay
no heed —
they give comfort and care and keep rain from
the seed
that would harvest the nightmares, the demons
and ghosts,
that seek to strangle, then lash you to gibbeting
post.
When all you need is someone to show they
care;
Say hi, be a friend and realise that you're there.

Drained

Green and purple, purple and green;
Do not tell the half of all you have seen.
Red and yellow, yellow and red;
Belie the truth of what you have said.
Beige and black, brown and blue;
Cannot paint a picture of all that is you.

All these colours in a rainbow go round
To paint façade that hides dark frown,
Shaped by anger at others you knew
And the fact that your mind tells you it's you.
So, the struggle and strife inside your head
Makes rubble from right you think wrong
instead.

Dawn

Nerves creep upwards now.
New start to old familiar.
Brings renewed vigour?

Build back, better?

8

Bold as brass
they learned fast
us distract
with false pact
and redrawn past
that covered cracks –
Our lives hacked.

Their greed recast.
We aghast;
raise white-flag mast.
They, so crass,
left love last,
devoured en masse –
Our lives pass.

Penance

Could we but reflect
On our world so imperfect
Would all genuflect?

There's too little time,
And we've no Maginot line.
"To heat or to dine?"

That is the question
That should force introspection,
Their dereliction.

"But where is the crime?"
Say sleek snakes greased in gold grime,
Counting growing dime.

Cos, what care rich few?
It's not thems that will turn blue;
Find peace at paid pew.

For the rest of us -
Who've got no hope, broken trust -
At least there's a bus!

Fare

"Some bread",
Hunger grumbled.

"Tough tread",
Lame stumbled.

"Better bred",
A Few snorted.

"Fat fed!"
Rich retorted.

"A bed…",
Cold begged.

Shame shed –
Blue neglect.

"Heavy head",
Tired minds ruminated.

"We're ahead",
Privilege profligated.

"Life bled",
Our hearts sighed.

Fast fled –
Our leaders lied.

"WORLD'S DEAD!"
Nature bellowed.

"Were wrong led"
Us, Hollow, echoed.

"Where's help?"
We, Lost, muted.

"At least we tried"
The brave dead saluted.

Token

A beat. (A knock. Contemplation.)

It's a good bag, seems strong, sturdy.
And you've got everything?
Enough t-shirts, jumpers, that extra towel?
Oh, the raincoat… Here it is.
See, rolls up nice and small, knew it would fit.
One last cuppa before you go?

A beat. (Step back. Disorientation.)

Your beard looks nice all trimmed and clean.
You've got that wash bag? The flask?
You're sure you've got enough?
Okay… right… I'm sorry… I'll desist.
Here, take these gloves… just to borrow.

A beat. (Step forward. Hesitation.)

Those boots scrub up well, they look good.
And you're wearing the thick socks.
They'll keep water out, they'll resist.
They'll be warm, if there's any snow…

A beat. (Stand still. Vacillation.)

You're sure I can't give you a hand?
Okay then, if you insist.
I'll wait downstairs, to see you go…

A beat. (Eyes down. Contrition.)

I'm sorry to do this.
I wish we could do more, you know…

A beat. (Door opens. Dereliction.)

Home?

No blacks, no dogs and no Irish,
But what is it that makes you British?

Be not judgemental, but be curious.
Stop staring at me and being envious.

Don't reject me for being Jew, Hindu, Muslim
Or being they/them, she/her, he/him

So don't push the prejudice of Pole, Paki, Pikey,
My tongues just as clear as any Scouse or
Geordie.

You see, I'm just like you, a hard-working
human;
I eat food, play sports, even listen to Ed Sheeran.

Don't mistakenly mirror my success
As some leg up akin to power and privilege.

I've got here because I am the greatest
Me. I'm living here, not invading your village.

I don't subscribe to your *veni, vidi, vici*.
I came, I saw, I conquered

Are slogans of ancient transgressor.
From Julius to William to House Hanover,
Did you know that all of us are from some
other?

So, forgive me if I start to sound bitchy;
This land is great because of its complexity.
A little respect's all I want you to give me…

Leader

A dark hue?
Welcome cue.
How you knew,
When so few
Could imbue
Feelings true.

Ward

Hear her tears
Once again
As her rain descends

Down on you
And on them
Onto no one who can save

Her child's life.

At least now
He is free
From this world in degradation.

Leaving her
You and me
Lost in thoughtless contemplation.

Living lives
Where we will be
Always fearing termination.

Stand tall, stand strong

Stand tall, stand strong, let them know you
belong.
Don't let them tell you what to do or say.
Fight for what's right, stand up against the
wrong.

Though the days come short, and the nights
grow long,
As long as there's light there'll be a next day.
Stand tall, stand strong, let them know you
belong.

Ignore false claims, and those ignorant songs,
Your life you defend – the truth they betray.
Fight for what's right, stand up against the
wrong.

Despite the odds, and doubts that you're not
strong,
All of this you can withstand – come what may.
Stand tall, stand strong, let them know you
belong.

It takes just one to cut a tear through the throng;
To rip out the rot, dispose of decay.
Fight for what's right, stand up against the
wrong.

What you do these days will other's hope
prolong.
You do what you must, there's no other way.
Stand tall, stand strong, let them know you
belong.
Fight for what's right, stand up against the
wrong!

Shelter

Her breasts stared back at me
As the baby suckled gently –
Not needing to pause for air
Nor the smothering smog I inhaled
From the black tracks of the subway
As dust shook from the ceiling above.

Her eyes glared blankly at me
As I finished another drag –
Stamping out the cigarette
She continued her mundane routine
Her breasts now judging me,
Nourishing life all the while.

A Ukrainian Football Fan's Chant!

Vladimir, Vladimir, Vladimir Putin
What an ego to commit such a sin!

Vladimir, Vladimir, Vladimir Putin
Knocked down our door but we won't let him
in!

Vladimir, Vladimir, Vladimir Putin
Not by the hairs on our chinny-chin-chin!

Vladimir, Vladimir, Vladimir Putin
We're our own people not your lost kin!

Vladimir, Vladimir, Vladimir Putin
Stark raving mad if you think you will win!

Vladimir, Vladimir, Vladimir Putin
Did you not know…we are Ukrainian!

Buried in Bucha

Ashen stalk
sticking out
from fresh dug ground.

Five vines sprout,
stretching out,
as if to try
and grasp the light,

or a future,

that was

Stolen.

If Seamus was a War-Correspondent.

Between his forefinger and his thumb
the squat pen rests; snug as a gun.

Beneath the window, a sharp rasping sound
as men drag metal across concreted ground:
one, Andriy, heaving. Seamus looks down

sees Andriy's strained strength amongst men no
more or less tough.
Hehaunches down, looks up ten years away,
sees a city coated in colour, glossed in glory,
where he was baking.

Large hands, softer than they look - than they
should -
deftly flick flour on worktop before rolling the
dough.
Light, malleable, ready for kneading
for baking, then for feeding – the body and soul
of customers who loved the cool hardness in
their hands.

By God, this good man could bake.
Just like his old man.

Then a light in the sky. A firework that terrifies.
And Andriy's back up, but soul is back down.
Strong, rigid, what the city's needing.
First welding - then piping - fresh-baked
hedgehogs
in decorative ring that stings the city's eyes;
seems to keep the light out, maintains life
within.
His hands, now not so soft.
Needing.
Kneading.

The warm smell of sulphur in the wet air, the
pop and flash
of anti-aircraft fire spotlighting the curt cuts of
an edge
of a city, roots still living, clinging, hoping…
Waiting
for a world too far from the terrors they'll one
day tell
and the reporter has no other way to try help.

Between his finger and his thumb
The squat pen rests.
He'll tell their tale with it.

Shadows

25

A vast congregation,
entrenched between benches.

A priest
scatterguns eulogies,
aimed at sainted sinners;
wise words for weapons,
so they can save their souls
from twisted,
conflicted
morals.

Woebegone winners –
the heavily wounded –
circumference the threshold
reciting an Apostles creed,
their mouths remain closed,
but souls
have been
freed.

Brave Few

26

If left only few,
Stood strong in yellow and blue,
What then would world do?